The Frequent Flyer's Practical Guide to Spiritual Travel

The Frequent Flyer's Practical Guide to Spiritual Travel:
Steps, Mistakes, and Successes in Following the Holy Spirit into Amazing Experiences
by La Vance Parris

ISBN-13: 9781732448674
ISBN-10: 1732448671

Copyright © 2019 La Vance Parris

Edited by Rachel Newman
Cover Design by Tyler Frick and Rachel Newman

Published by Lazarus Tribe Media, LLC
Rome, Georgia

All rights reserved. No part of this book may be reproduced or transmitted in any form by any means, electronic, mechanical, photocopy, recording or other without the prior written permission of the publisher.

Scripture quotations are from the KING JAMES VERSION (KJV): KING JAMES VERSION, public domain.

Printed in the United States of America.

Publisher's Site: www.lazarustribemedia.com
Author's Page: www.lazarustribemedia.com/lavanceparris

The
Frequent Flyer's Practical Guide
to
Spiritual Travel:
Steps, Mistakes, and Successes in Following the Holy Spirit into Amazing Experiences

by La Vance Parris

Lazarus Tribe Media
Rome, Georgia

To the Holy Spirit, the Greatest Teacher of all. The One who guides me into all truth. The One who gives me the utterance to pray out the plan of God for my life, brings all things to my remembrance, and shows me the future. You are indeed my Helper, my Comforter my Counselor, my Intercessor, my Advocate, my Standby, and my Strengthener.

To my grandmother, Daisy Foney, whose love for her Heavenly Father imprinted my heart. She was not ashamed to let the Holy Spirit have control over her body as she danced under the power of the anointing in that little country church. As a little girl, her obedience caused me to stand in awe of the power and presence of God.

Special Thanks

Special thanks to my loving husband, Charles, who has kept his promise to show me his God. Thank you so much for taking me by the hand and teaching me those things that the Holy Spirit taught you. Thank you for believing in me, being patient, and constantly telling me, "You can do it!" You are the one man that I have the utmost respect for and confidence in because I have seen first-hand the love and the relationship you have with your God. By sharing your experiences with God, you have caused me and others to know that we can have that personal relationship with Father also.

To Lee Frost, Pastor of Harvest Life Church in Talladega, Alabama. Thank you for staying current with the Holy Spirit, having an ear to hear what He is saying, and not being afraid to speak even when it is not the norm. You did not know that the word you spoke in my life confirmed what God had already spoken to me. It caused me to press into the deeper things of God. I am forever grateful.

A special thanks to Aaron Parris who is always willing to take time out of his busy schedule to listen to me. No matter if I was excited about a new revelation, a new experience, or just plain frustrated, Aaron, you were always willing to help me. And if anything was questionable, you used your research abilities to find truth. I could not have made it without you. You are truly amazing!

A special thanks Aleta Jennings for I am thankful God put you in my life. You are strong in the areas I am weak. Thank you for being so willing to strengthen my words.

To my Church family who stood by me and did not say, "You are crazy," but instead, "How do I make it work in my life?" Thank you for believing in me.

To Rachel Newman of Lazarus Tribe Media of Rome, Georgia. You were God's divine connection. You have been so patient in helping me to publish this book. It certainly would not have happened without your help and encouragement. Thank you so much for all you have done to finish the first part of this project.

Table of Contents

Foreword	11
Introduction	13
Special People, Special Assignments, Special Seasons	17
Flying Foretold	21
Focus and Pay Attention	25
Trial and Error	29
Learning to Fly	33
Salvation on Death Row	37
Completed Assignments	41
Time Travel	45
Purging Pride	47
Hunger for More of God	49
Out of Body/In Body	51
No Fear In Love	55
The Unknown	57
Frequently Asked Questions	61
Testimonies From Others	65
Prayer and Activation	69
List of Referenced Scriptures	72
Personal Journal Entries	75

Foreword

I know the subjects of "translation," "out of the body experiences," and even "being in the Spirit," are not commonplace today. Still, there are those who will tell you they have had these experiences. My wife, La Vance, is one of those people. She has not been translated (traveled in the Spirit) once or twice, but many times over. Her experiences open up a new frontier in the world of the Spirit and she shares it in the pages of this book.

La Vance has always desired the deeper, beyond-the-normal things of God. The operation of the gifts of the Spirit, a glory cloud, a vision or anything that has to do with the moving of God's Spirit fascinates her. And she has a desire for that which is only shared by a few chosen. Yes, I suppose you would place her in the class of the "radical seekers." Those who seek after the deep things of the Kingdom of God. She says, "I want to know and do the things of the Bible. I want them operating in my life, and I want to teach others how to do the same."

La Vance came to the Extended Hand Church while she was a college student at Jacksonville State University (JSU). JSU is located in the city of Jacksonville, Alabama, which is the neighboring city of mine and La Vance's home, Piedmont, Alabama. She was not only a young JSU student, she was also a student of God's Word. She was full of questions--not ordinary questions. She wanted to know the details of how everything in the Bible worked!

It was useless to simply say, "It works by the Spirit." Her next question would be, "But how do I make it work in my life?" Believe you me I know because I spent hours as her pastor trying to answer her questions. And if I was successful, she would then say, "Teach me how to do it. I want it." This happened regularly during the Monday night prayer meeting at Extended Hand Church. Monday nights were a time of prayer and teaching of the Word. La Vance always made sure she got her questions in the mix of the lesson for the night. She grew in faith and knowledge of the Lord Jesus Christ, and the Great Holy Spirit became her Teacher and Guide. He then led her into things which are not common to the average church member. When she received the prophecy that she would be a "frequent flyer," I told her that the Holy Spirit would fly with her and teach her and she, in turn, would teach others. That is what this book is about. She has tapped into one of the unpracticed truths of God's Word. A casual reader might read over the truth of translation, not La Vance Parris. Because of her unique experiences, she has searched the Scriptures concerning the subject. She has proven by the Scriptures that God does translate people.

Not only that, she has prayed untold hours concerning the subject. And because of her diligent searching, God has allowed her to be a leader on the frontier of translation. She has dared to walk where few have walked, and now wants to share her experiences with those who have the same adventurous desires--desires to truly go to the highest height in the realms of the Spirit. This book is written to share her experiences and teach others the "How To's" of "Spiritual Flying."

So, for me, it is with no small measure of expectation of what reading this book may do and how it may affect you in your experiences with God. Read it slowly, meditate on it, and walk out what God teaches you through it. And who knows, you may find yourself in some far away dungeon or prison ministering to some hurting and forgotten individual, and at the same time meet the author of this book because she really is a frequent flyer!

Charles Parris
Pastor of Extended Hand Church
Piedmont, Alabama

Introduction

After receiving Jesus as her personal Savior, the woman immediately sat up in the bed, wrapped her arms around me tightly and began to sob uncontrollably. I knew that she realized she had just been forgiven. The blood of Jesus washed away her sins.

I could tell that her heart was deeply broken. The right side of her face was touching mine as she hugged me.

She whispered in my right ear, "I didn't mean to kill her."

I said, "I know you didn't, and Jesus doesn't hold it against you."

She held me what seemed like a few minutes, and there was so much accomplished in that hug. She had experienced God's amazing love and forgiveness.

What a deep heartfelt experience! God used me to travel in the Spirit to rescue someone who was about to die on death row and go to a devil's hell! This is what can happen when we surrender ourselves to the leadership of the Holy Spirit. He wants to use us. He wants us to yield ourselves completely to His service.

My husband always says, "A revelation is your invitation to experience the fullness of that revelation." In other words, if you can see it you can have it.

Some of my first translation experiences, also called traveling in the Spirit, were back in the 1990s. I did not know at that time they were actually designed as an invitation for me to enter into the fullness of this truth.

Once I found myself flying with a commercial aircraft. As strange as it may sound, I know it happened. I had my hands on the plane, but I was not dependent on the plane for my flight. I had somehow simply joined myself to it.

What I want you to understand is, it was a real-life experience.

The wind blowing on my face, my hands touching the plane, and me praying in tongues made me know without any doubt I was really flying alongside a plane. I even said to myself, "Lord, I am flying alongside this plane!"

> "A revelation is your invitation to experience the fullness of that revelation."

The next experience early in my travels began as I saw myself walking into a room. I thought I was having a dream. The room had twin beds, one bed on the right and one on the left. Two children, both around the age of seven years old, lie on the bed on the right. Somehow, I knew they had been left alone. Their little faces told me they were afraid. I pulled the cover up on them and tucked them in. I then sat on the other bed and prayed in tongues. I do not know if I was speaking their language or not, but it seemed they understood me because they were comforted as I prayed.

Soon, I knew they were okay, and my attention was drawn to a voice. I could hear someone from a distance praying in tongues. Then, I understood I was actually moving toward the sound of the voice. I know it is hard to believe, but as I drew closer, I knew the person praying in tongues was me.

I cannot explain that, I only know it happened.

Then suddenly I was back in my room.

I became conscious of my body as my right leg entered my body, which caused me to shiver. I said, "Oh, that's weird." Up until this point, I would have thought I was dreaming. But the feeling I had as I re-entered my body convinced me it was much more than just a dream.

This event caused me to wonder if the Lord had used other people in similar ways and they also thought it was only a dream. I wish that I had known at that time that this was my invitation to come into the fullness of this revelation of traveling in the Spirit, but I did not. I thought at the most it might happen maybe once or twice in a lifetime. Therefore, I did not know to pursue it.

I later discovered a Scripture where Jesus said those born of the Spirit are "like the wind."

> *The wind bloweth where it listeth, and thou hearest the sound thereof, but canst not tell whence it cometh, and whither it goeth: so is every one that is born of the Spirit. John 3:8*

That Scripture seemed to settle things for me, and bring an assurance I was truly being used of God rather than getting off course into error.

Dear Reader, God's love is so great He is willing to do the extraordinary to help those who are hurting. He is looking for those who are willing to be used in the unbelievable and unthinkable ways in order to rescue those who need Him.

My desire, and I believe it is also God's desire, for this book is to make people aware of this awesome, God-given ability. My experiences will cause others to desire the same. Please know this book is serving you as an invitation to come into this revelation. All you have to do is pursue Him with all your heart, believe what the Word of God says about you, and I know you will come into the fullness of it.

Many might ask, "Are there Biblical examples of anyone being translated?" The answer is yes. There are more accounts than one would think. The most familiar one is when Phillip was sent to minister to the Ethiopian Eunuch. He found him in the desert, riding in a chariot, reading from the book of Isaiah. After explaining to the Eunuch the Scripture he was reading, Philip then baptized him.

The Bible says,

> "And when they were come up out of the water, the Spirit of the Lord caught away Philip, that the eunuch saw him no more: and he went on his way rejoicing. But Philip was found at Azotus:..."
> Acts 8:39-40

Azotus was about 34 miles from where the baptism took place. Philip had been supernaturally translated there. The Bible contains several other accounts that validate this truth.

1

Special People
Special Assignments
Special Seasons

In a night vision, I saw the hand of God write, "Special people have special assignments in special seasons." I knew that it was not only a message to me, but also to the Body of Christ.

Body of Christ, do you know that you are a special people, a peculiar people? If not, then Father desires for you to come to the understanding that you are indeed a special people.

> *"For thou art an holy people unto the Lord thy God: the Lord thy God hath chosen thee to be a special people unto himself, above all people that are upon the face of the earth." Deuteronomy 7:7*

The word "special" means to be distinguished by some unusual quality; especially, to be held in particular esteem, designed for a particular purpose or occasion.

Do you know, child of God, that God has a purpose for your life? God told Jeremiah,

> "Before I formed thee in the belly I knew thee; and before thou camest forth out of the womb I sanctified thee, and I ordained thee a prophet unto the nations." Jeremiah 1:5

Did you grasp that statement?

"BEFORE I formed thee in the belly I KNEW THEE; and BEFORE thou CAMEST FORTH out of the womb I SANCTIFIED THEE, and ORDAINED THEE a prophet unto the nations."

God sanctified Jeremiah and ordained him a prophet to the nations before he was born. How awesome is that to know that God also knew you and had a plan for your life mapped out before you were born! Yes, you are a special person with a special assignment for a special season.

You may be asking, "what is an assignment?" An assignment is a specified task or amount of work assigned or undertaken as if assigned by authority. An assignment may also be a position, post, or office to which one is assigned.

Your next questions is likely, "how do I find out my assignment?" First, I would get to know the One Who is to give me my assignments. Then, I would ask Him!

When I understand my assignment, I would make sure that I carry out my assignment to completion. An assignment can be as simple as baking someone a cake, writing someone a letter, calling someone on the phone to give them a word from the Lord, or praying for a sick person in the hospital.

Ananias had an assignment. In fact, the name "Ananias" means "whom God has graciously given."

> "And there was a certain disciple at Damascus, named Ananias; and to him said the Lord in a vision, Ananias. And he said, Behold, I am here, Lord. And the Lord said unto him, Arise and go into the street which is called Straight, and enquire in the house of Judas for one called Saul, of Tarsus: for, behold, he prayeth, And hath seen in a vision a man name Ananias coming in, and putting his hand on him, that he might receive his sight." Acts 9:10-12

Please note that God is working on both ends. He's giving Ananias instructions in a vision, and also gave Saul a vision of Ananias coming to him and putting his hand on him. Why did God do that? I believe God chose to prepare both of them so that the assignment would be completed.

> "Then Ananias answered, Lord, I have heard by many of this man, how much evil he hath done to thy saints at Jerusalem: And here he hath authority from the chief priests to bind all that call on thy name." Acts 9:13-14

Ananias seems to have struggled with fear while God prepared him for the task. I wonder how many times the enemy has stopped us from entering our assignment by reminding us of what others have done to us, or by telling us that we cannot do it. How many opportunities have we missed to minister to people because we were distracted by how we'd been treated in the past?

> "But the Lord said unto him, Go thy way: for he is a chosen vessel unto me, to bear my name before the Gentiles, and kings, and the children of Israel:" Acts 9:15

In order to fulfill your assignments, you must hear the voice of God above all other voices. To try and prevent you from taking a first step, the enemy may remind you of negative things others have said or done. He will lie to you and attempt to discourage you.

> "For I will shew him how great things he must suffer for my name's sake. And Ananias went his way, and entered into the house; and putting his hands on him said, Brother Saul, the Lord, even Jesus, that appeared unto thee in the way as thou camest, hath sent me, that thou mightiest receive thy sight, and be filled with the Holy Ghost. And immediately there fell from his eyes as it had been scales: and he received sight forthwith, and arose, and was baptized." Acts 9:16-18

How many of you know that there is more along the way?

First, God told Ananias that Saul saw him coming to lay hands on him that he might receive his sight. But, somewhere along the way, further instructions were given that Saul would be filled with the Holy Ghost.

You must step out to find out.

Why would God give you His whole plan if you are not willing to follow the first instruction?

> *"You must hear the voice of God above all other voices."*

Arise and go.

> "And he said, The God of our fathers hath chosen thee, that thou shouldest know his will, and see that Just One, and shouldest hear the voice of his mouth. For thou shalt be his witness unto all men of what thou hast seen and heard. And now why tarriest thou? Arise, and be baptized, and wash away thy sins, calling on the name of the Lord" Acts 22: 14-16

I believe there are people crying out as Saul did, "Lord, what would you have me to do?" And I believe that God has those who, like Ananias, will be the one "whom God has graciously given" to speak into someone's life.

Are you ready for your assignment? Are you willing to take the first step? Are you willing to forget about what others have said about the people you are being sent to and listen only to the Voice of God? For those very people could be a chosen vessel unto the Lord!

Get to know the One Who knows the plans that He has for you. For you are indeed a special people who have special assignments in special seasons. Be ready to be used by Him however He chooses. Arise and go whether in the body or out of the body!

2

Flying Foretold

On a beautiful Fall day in September, we attended a tent meeting in Jacksonville, Alabama to celebrate "Sukkot," also known as "The Feast of Tabernacles." This Fall feast is the seventh and final festival celebrated by the people of Israel. It is a Jewish custom to build small "sukkah huts" in which meals are eaten throughout this week-long festival. These dwellings are a reminder of those in which Israel lived during their 40-year sojourn in the wilderness after the exodus from bondage in Egypt.

With great anticipation I was looking forward to attending the meeting because I had never celebrated the Feast of Tabernacles. What would I see? What would we do? What would it entail?

We left my house in Piedmont and drove south on Highway 21. Anticipation grew mile by mile for about twelve miles. We turned right onto a country road called Roy Webb Road. We drove about three miles deeper into the country before turning left onto a dirt road. I eagerly took in the scenery, still wondering what this biblical feast would involve.

As we topped the hill, I could see an herb farm surrounded by agricultural land. There was a small-framed, white house and a shed, which housed a tractor used for cultivating the land. I also saw a dairy cow grazing in the pasture and a few chickens pecking for food. Finally, I saw a small, white tent standing in the open field.

Under the tent, everything was in order. The stage was set with the pulpit centered in the front. A piece of carpet laid in front of the stage, and an aisle down the middle separated two sections of chairs, which faced the pulpit. There was enough seating for about fifty people (tightly). A few picnic tables prepared with the Feast meal sat to the right of that little white tent.

After greeting everyone as they arrived, we sat down for the Feast meal. Our hearts filled with thanksgiving as the meal began. We thanked the Lord for everything He had done for us. We thanked Him for being our substitute for sin. We thanked Him for willingly laying down His life for us so that we could have eternal life. We thanked Him for taking the stripes on His back for our healing. Such an awesome presence of the Lord surrounded those picnic tables! Then we prayed, blessed the food, and began to partake.

I was somewhat disappointed in the meal. We had what I recognized to be barbecue sandwiches. It may have been lamb, but I did not ask. I had expected a Jewish atmosphere, with a setting that would remind you of the traveling Israelites. I also expected the shofar to be blown to bring all the people in to be served lamb cooked on an open fire with bitter herbs. Not even one person was dressed in traditional Jewish attire. No one even spoke of the meaning of the feast. In my opinion, the menu was an American meal, so my expectations were not fulfilled as far as the natural meal was concerned. However, my thoughts quickly moved past that because the food was quite filling.

As we sat around the tables fellowshipping with one another, one of the young ladies suddenly pointed saying, "Look at that!"

It was as though the Lord had shown up with a gift for us all. A beautiful painting! It was as though an artist had used the heavens for a canvas and painted the most beautiful masterpiece I had ever seen!

I saw a perfect picture of a castle with the old English features. A golden driveway led right up to the door from the horizon at the edge of the pasture. Only the hand of God could have created such beauty with the clouds! When I first looked, I thought it was someone's real fortress on earth.

What was God saying with this panorama in the sky? Perhaps He said, "I am here, not to dwell in castles of wood and stone, but in mansion of My Father's house."

As magnificent as that cloud arrangement was (and I think it speaks of the best earth could produce), it did not compare to the mansions in which He desired to fully dwell (John 14:2).

The congregation at the Feast arose and walked away from the picnic tables to stare at the magnificent scene. Some of the viewers did not seem to see or appreciate the beautiful scene that Father had displayed for us. They did not seem to have an eye to see what others were seeing. They only saw colorful clouds. But to those that had an eye to see, the view of the castle astounded them. My words fail me to describe this beautifully detailed scene! I have yet to figure out how it related to the Feast of Tabernacles, but that glorious scene will forever be imprinted in my mind.

The heavenly picture faded away, the meal ended, and the main service began. I could feel the Presence of God as the people united in worshipful singing. The Lord's Presence was so tangible I thought the King had left His throne to come meet with a few people under a little white tent. I do not remember what the speaker taught that night. However, I do remember the thought of being in the right place at the right time, in the very presence of the King of Kings.

After the speaker finished the message, Charles, my husband, was asked to minister to the people. He began to speak prophetically to a lady from Hokes Bluff, Alabama. The Spirit of God told her that she was going to be a "frequent flyer" in the spirit realm.

Charles then turned to me and said, "That belongs to you also."

When he said that to me, I thought, "Frequent flyer?" What did this mean? I thought of Delta Airlines' Frequent Flyer program, which offers rewards for re-occurring use of their airline. Did it mean I was going to be spending more time at the airports of the world? Would I be flying to many different countries and I would be deemed a frequent flyer? I think I wanted that to be true. At first I couldn't let myself believe God was saying I would be flying as in translation to the point God would call me a frequent flyer.

Don't get me wrong, I believe in prophecy. But there was an argument going on inside of me between my spirit and my soul. My soul did not want to believe, but my spirit refused to doubt the prophecy. I knew God had spoken, but what was He really saying to me?

Maybe it meant I would be translated by the Spirit of God frequently like the characters in the Bible? Would I know ahead of time I was going, and would I know where I was going?

Those questions, among many others, buzzed in my head. Of course, I knew the Bible record of those who were translated, like Philip and Ezekiel, but what was God saying to me personally?

How could I activate this prophecy in my life?

First, I received it as a true word from God to me, then I prayed and laid it up in my heart, not knowing that the prophetic word would later be confirmed.

Prayer Meeting in Talladega, Alabama

Our church is affiliated with a few churches that meet every Monday for a time of prayer, sharing the Word of God, and fellowship. We rotate weekly from church to church. Harvest Assembly of Talladega, Alabama hosted the meeting on this particular Monday. A small crowd of about fifteen people gathered to pray. The host pastor, Lee Frost, turned to me while speaking and said, "Sister La Vance, the Lord just told me to tell you that you are going to travel in the Spirit like John G. Lake and minister to people."

Pastor Frost did not know that he had just confirmed the prophecy I received 6 months earlier under the tent at the Feast of Tabernacles.

I said, "Thank You, Jesus," and just laid it up in my heart.

I had heard about John G. Lake and knew him as an awesome man of God. He was a Canadian-American leader in the Pentecostal movement that began in the early 20th century. He is known as a faith-healer and missionary. I had read of his translation experiences in his book, "Adventures in God." The book truly inspired me as a believer, and made me hunger for the deeper things of God. Now, I had received a prophecy comparing my future experiences of traveling in the Spirit with his! I knew the first thing I must do was receive the prophecy as the Word of God to me. So, I said, "Lord, I receive this as You speaking directly to me."

My words did not seem to be enough. I knew I needed help with this one, so I went to the One who knows about those things: My Teacher, the Holy Spirit. I knew He would help me to pray the right prayer about it. The next several months were filled with hours of praying in the Spirit. Many times I would just awaken during the night even if I had been in bed only two or three hours. I knew God wanted me to meet Him in prayer, so I would slip out of bed and go to my prayer room. There my hunger was only momentarily filled. I just could not get enough of God. What had been hard became easier. In the beginning I had to make myself pray in the Spirit, but now I knew I had a destiny and a purpose. Each night I drew closer to it.

3

Focus and Pay Attention

The Helicopter

One night before going to bed, several months after Pastor Frost prophesied that I would travel in the Spirit in the manner of John G. Lake, I knelt in my bedroom praying when the Holy Spirit reminded me of the prophecy of being a "Frequent Flyer."

I said to the Lord, "Lord, I remember those prophecies spoken over me. Therefore, anytime You want to use me, body, soul, and spirit, or only spirit and soul, I submit myself to Your Spirit. Use me if You will." I got up off the floor and went to bed.

While lying there in the dark with my eyes shut, I suddenly heard the sound of a helicopter. I thought to myself, "I hear a helicopter." Then, I could feel the swaying from side to side. It was as though I was actually flying in a helicopter. (I knew how it felt to fly in a helicopter because my husband and I had flown in one on our honeymoon.) Several seconds passed, then I opened my eyes and saw a beautiful blue sky. The sight scared me, and I quickly shut my eyes again.

As I shut my eyes, I began to descend. I was falling out of the sky at a very fast rate of speed. Falling so fast! Almost like being in a car, I tried to apply brakes to myself to soften my fall.

Suddenly, I could feel myself as I went back into my body.

As I lay there thinking about how quickly God answered my prayer for Him to use me, I awed at what I just experienced! He answered my prayer immediately!

However, I felt upset at the same time. I disappointed myself by abruptly closing my eyes in fear. If I want to see something in the natural realm and close my eyes, I will never see it. Well, the same goes in the spiritual: to see the things of God you must be looking.

I talked to my husband about closing my eyes, and he helped me to understand that God was not mad at me. He said, "God knew you would close your eyes before you ever flew. Take a spiritual note of it, and next time keep your eyes open, see where you are going, and see what Father wants you to see."

He seemed to think my mishap that night was funny, but I did not think so. He seemed to know with confidence that Father would give me another chance. I had an assignment, but I aborted it by allowing fear to take hold of me. Through this experience I learned that I must keep my eyes open to see what Father would have me to see.

The Next Time

My husband was right. There was a next time.

A few nights later, while I was lying on my stomach in bed, I suddenly felt my spirit come out of my body. I hovered up in the air about three feet. I was shocked to see my body still on the bed by my husband! I realized I was about to travel in the Spirit somewhere, but then I heard my sleeping husband snore, and my mind went to him. In that instant, my spirit slammed back into my body.

> "To see the things of God you must be looking."

I heard the Spirit say, "Focus and pay attention."

This trip was short. Perhaps I cannot even call it a trip, maybe an "experience." But at any rate, I did learn from it. I understood then that my soul (which is my mind, will, and emotions) could be distracted and cause my trip to be terminated immediately. I knew that I couldn't allow anything to make me lose focus.

I felt so disappointed in myself because I knew I failed again. God wanted to use me, but I did not know what to do. I did not know how to function outside of my body. I could feel fear rising up in me. It was as though I was a child beginning to walk for the first time, not sure whether I would fall or not, unstable in my maneuvering.

Oh, how I desperately needed the Holy Spirit to teach me!

I repented again and spent days praying in the Spirit, and asking the Holy Spirit to teach me how to function outside of my body in a way pleasing to God.

My husband had told me to keep spiritual notes of what happens during these experiences, the successes as well as the failures. So, my spiritual notebook began to fill up. I had so much to learn and no one to talk to about these things, which made my desire to be in my prayer room overwhelming. I simply could not wait for those special times alone with the Holy Spirit.

4

Trial and Error

Missions Aborted

In the beginning, I aborted several missions due to fear and a lack of understanding. I wanted so much to get it right! Each experience became a classroom of meditation.

On one occasion, I entered an ambulance in route to the hospital. I saw the attendants as they tried desperately to keep the person alive. After only a few seconds, I allowed fear to overtake me and I came out.

Another time, the Spirit carried me to a wooded area. I did not see anyone from my secluded position, but understood a meeting was taking place. I could hear the chanting of what I thought to be a group of witches. Unfortunately, fear won again and I terminated the mission.

I aborted each mission because of fear. I knew I must conquer fear.

But how?

The Word of God had to become the foundation on which I stood. Therefore, I meditated on 2 Timothy 1:7,

> *"For God hath not given us the spirit of fear, but of power, and of love and of a sound mind."*

I turned that Scripture over and over in my spirit. I confessed it several times a day. John 1 tells us that the Word became flesh, so I knew my flesh had to become Word. In other words, my flesh had to become what the Word says it is.

Night After Night I Hoped

Night after night, I went to bed with hope that each night would be the night God would once again choose to let me go somewhere. Where He chose to take me did not matter to me. I expected, waited, desired. I just wanted to go.

ICU

Then, the next experience came, but this time it was different. I did not know when I left my body, I simply arrived at my destination, and stood at a wall. Without thinking, I stepped forward through the wall and found myself in a hospital's Intensive Care Unit. I saw a person lying on a bed, wearing an oxygen mask. He or she, I could not tell which, remained alive via a life support system.

I felt fear, again, and drew back.

My drawing back caused me to fall at a tremendous rate of speed. I do not know how to explain it, but I found my "brakes." Like applying brakes on a car, I slowed my fall. Each time I applied the brakes, I tempered my fall until I came to a complete stop. Then, in a twinkling of an eye, I was back in my body.

I laid there feeling so disgusted with myself.

Again, I felt I cut my mission short because of fear. I went to my prayer room to pray for that person in the ICU. I really didn't know how to pray, so I asked the Holy Spirit to help me pray, and He did. He anointed me to pray in English, and after doing so, I spent more time praying in the Spirit (in tongues) also.

I do not know if I will ever learn what happened to that person, but I do believe that the Holy Spirit helped me to pray for them. (As I think back now, I believe the purpose of the mission was to pray for that person in ICU.)

Spiritual flying was still new to me. I understood little about it, but I intended to learn quickly. God continued to teach me, one mission at a time, and I did my best to learn.

I purposed in my heart that the next time I traveled I would keep my eyes open and be obedient to God without fear. I also made up my mind to pray in the Spirit as often as I could. That meant if I went to the store down the street, which would take 15 minutes, or visited another city 45 minutes away, I prayed in tongues all the way there and back.

I prayed in tongues while washing dishes and cleaning house. I prayed in tongues in my prayer closet. I prayed in tongues to the point I think I was pushing hard on Apostle Paul's record of "praying in tongues more than you all" (See 1 Corinthians 14:18). I wanted the Holy Spirit to teach me everything available to learn about this type of travel.

> "I also made up my mind to pray in the Spirit as often as I could."

Hole in the Wall

The next mission came after weeks of praying in the Spirit and waiting. I rested in bed awake and began seeing a vision of a boat. As I focused on this boat, I felt my spirit come up out of my body. I quickly remembered that I must keep my eyes open, so I opened my eyes. To my surprise, I saw the tops of trees. I flew over land, then above a body of water, and then my spirit shot horizontally like a rocket. I started to pray in the Spirit. (That's right, I prayed in the Spirit while having an out-of-body experience! During this mission, my understanding increased with this revelation: we have the ability to pray in the Spirit while traveling in the Spirit! Apostle Paul said in 1 Corinthians 14:14, "It is my spirit that prays." This is a great revelation to know.)

I suddenly stopped and stood by a rock wall. The wall had a hole that looked to be about the size of a manhole like you might see in the streets of big cities. Then, a second later, I stood on the other side of the wall looking back at the hole as it filled with a rock-like material similar to that of the wall. The filling fit like a piece of a puzzle. Once in place, I could not tell there had been a hole in the wall at all. I sensed that I entered a secret place beyond the wall.

As I stood watching, I felt someone take me by my shoulders to turn me around. Thinking it was my husband, I said, "No, wait! I must watch this wall." Then, I felt someone wrap their arms around my legs just above my knees. However, I did not discern that I should turn around and look down to see who wanted my attention. At the time, I thought my assignment was to watch the wall.

The next thing I knew, I was falling out of the sky and hitting my brakes to slow me down. Then, I was back in my body.

As I laid in my bed and thought about what just happened, I still felt the hand on my shoulder…

This experience truly moved me. I felt extremely ignorant because I did not turn around to see who grabbed me.

I failed again in the mission. I thought, "Surely God must be so disappointed in me!" So, I went back to my prayer room to ask God to forgive me.

As I meditated on what happened to me during the mission, questions flooded my mind. Who was the person that tried to turn me around? Was it a child that wrapped their arms around my legs? Did they know I was there to help them? Were they being held captive? How could I have helped them? God, why did you send me there? I wanted answers! I desperately wanted to successfully complete the missions God had for me.

Back in my prayer room:

I remembered that I had been taught I am a triune person. I am not going to be a spirit when I die, I am a spirit right now. I live in a body, and I have a soul. My soul is my mind, will, and emotions. I knew my problem was with my soul. Somehow I must get my soul-man to stay in submission to my spirit-man. To do so, it would have to be renewed by the Word of God to know what is that perfect will of God concerning these things (Roman 12:1-2). I knew this concerning other things, now I am learning my mind must be trained by the Holy Spirit to agree with my own spirit. My spirit would go back into my body every time I doubted, lost focus, or began to fear, think ahead, or even if I looked away from what God was showing me.

I cried out again to the Holy Spirit to teach me how to function out of my body. I knew in time I would surely be able to distinguish between being in or out of my body.

Therefore, I continued to pray in the Spirit concerning these things.

5

Learning to Fly

The Prisoner

The next time, I left my body without knowing. I simply became aware of myself walking on a path. I instinctively knew where to go. I drew near to a group of about seven men. They stood just outside of the place that I knew I needed to go. The men wore tan uniforms similar to those I have seen janitors wear. I knew they were guards of some sort. Everything about these men spoke of trouble and I did not want to go past them. I noticed that one of them was smoking a cigarette.

Then I had a soulish thought, "You don't want to go past them."

At that point, I stepped back two or three steps. I knew that I was about to return to my body. But I stopped and said, "No, God has not given me a spirit of fear, but of power, and of love, and of a sound mind!" A peace and a boldness came over me. I walked right beside them and noticed that they did not see me. I kept walking until I got to the door of the place I was to enter. I noticed large, decorative letters on the right side of the wall: "PCS."

I knew every step and every turn as though I was pre-programmed which way to go. The dungeon-like building contained long and narrow halls. I walked through a tunnel, past walls of cement and dirt, to my destination.

I arrived in a room similar to a jail cell. The beds looked much like bunk beds. A man laid on the top bed. Somehow, I noticed everything about him, even that he was not fully dressed. When he saw me, he raised up on his elbow. This amazed me because the men outside did not see me.

He stared at me as if he beheld a heavenly being.

I said to him, "Sir, Jesus has forgiven you for what you did to your sister."

I know my words deeply touched him because tears welled up in his eyes and ran down his face. I continued with my message to him by saying, "but you must trust Jesus, and He will help you."

I asked him if he wanted to accept Jesus as his Savior, and he nodded his head, "yes." I then reached over, laid my hand on his hand, and said, "Repeat this prayer after me." As I prayed, the prisoner repeated every word. He became free from sin as God miraculously forgave and saved him!

I don't know how I appeared to the man as I walked into his cell, but I could tell by his staring eyes that he could not believe what he saw.

How awesome! God did not expose the man's sin. I do not know what he had done to his sister. I only knew that God had given me a word of knowledge to help the man, so he could know how much God loved him and would forgive him. The man repented. God had saved this poor man!

I finished my assignment! As I took my hand off of his, I looked into his eyes and took a step backwards.

At the snap of a finger, I entered another place. It was so beautiful! Flowers covered the landscape. As I beheld the beautiful sight, I heard a voice speak two words: "Asia and Mullock." (To this day, I do not know what those words meant or how they related to my assignment.) Then, I began my descent, falling and hitting my brakes, and I was back in my body.

I rejoiced that I finally completed my assignment! I did not give in to fear. I had started to learn how to operate outside of my body. Thank you, Jesus! The feeling of success overwhelmed me.

I know I will see that man from the jail cell in heaven. "For God is not willing that any should perish, but for all to come to repentance" (See 2 Peter 3:9). God's love is real. He loves us with an everlasting love. He will send someone to the ends of the Earth just to give someone else the opportunity to receive Him as Savior. I am so thankful that I finally was beginning to get it right!

Deliverance in the Red-Light District

On the evening of the 2012 Presidential Election, I went to bed exhausted, not thinking about the possibility of being translated. All of a sudden, I noticed that I was out of my body in flight to an unknown place. I saw houses below and lights shining in the distance. Immediately, I stood in front of an apartment building. I looked to the right and to the left. I asked myself, "Which way do I go?" I then knew to go to the right.

The place looked much like the red-light districts you see on TV. People went in and out of the apartment building. I saw the people, but they could not see me. The front of the building was open and did not have any doors. The opening was a passageway with rooms on each side. I entered the building and slowly and cautiously walked down the passageway.

This was a place I would normally not want to be in. The atmosphere caused me to hesitate to go any farther. I did not like what I was feeling. Fear began to overpower me and I had the familiar feeling of falling.

Seconds later, the passageway disappeared. I now saw a blurry darkness as if something was passing by me at a high rate of speed. I knew from previous experiences, the mission was being aborted. I did not want that to happen! So, I resisted with everything within me and cried out, "No!"

My resistance and declaration reversed everything and I stood in the hallway once again. I thought to myself, "I just reversed everything by resisting the fall!" Another lesson learned! What I mean by resisting is, it felt as though someone pushed up against me, trying to push me out of the mission. Therefore, I pushed back with all my might and won the victory. I had defeated the aborting powers.

Back in the passageway of the apartment building, I noticed the doors on both sides had little triangle-shaped windows. They all looked alike.

I asked, "Which door, Father?"

He answered by giving me an open vision: I saw a light shining in one of the windows, and I knew He had marked that door for me. I walked down the hall checking each door for a light, but saw only darkness.

Then, a young girl, who appeared to be about 15 years old, came along beside me and asked, "Who are you looking for?"

"I'll know it when I see it," I replied.

The teenager tagged along with me. We passed more doors and then turned a corner. There was the door! It looked just like Father had shown me in the vision! The light-marked door had a picture stuck in the bottom portion of the window. I pulled it off to take a closer look and realized it was a photo of the young girl who joined me in the hallway.

In amazement, I turned to her and said, "You're the one! You're the one I am to pray for!" I put the picture back in its place in the little window.

She seemed to submit to my words and sat down on an old lounge chair near us in the hallway. As I began praying for her, a demon manifested through her and caused her to twist, squirm, and growl. At that point, I spoke to the devil and said, "Come out of her. You have no choice, but to come out of her in the Name of Jesus!"

Finally, she relaxed, indicating to me she was delivered. She looked at me as if to say, "what happened?" A change in her countenance with a smile on her face, and her thankfulness let me know that she was set free.

> "And these signs shall follow them that believe; In my name shall they cast out devils..." Mark 16:17

Immediately, I felt that falling-out-of-the-sky feeling and arrived back in my body. Once again, the Lord had transported my spirit to an unknown place. This time, He sent me to minister deliverance to someone held captive by demons!

6

Salvation on Death Row

"Then the same day at evening, being the first day of the week, when the doors were shut where the disciples were assembled for fear of the Jews, came Jesus and stood in the midst ...." John 20:19

Even though I still felt moments of fear, I would not give into it. I would still declare that God has not given me the spirit of fear, but of power, and of love, and a sound mind (2 Timothy 1:7).

During this experience, I did not know I had left my body. I stepped through a wall and stood at the left side of a bed. I saw a woman in the bed. I noticed that the left side of her face was disfigured. She looked depressed and filled with hopelessness.

Again, I did not have to think about what to say. I opened my mouth and words just came out. This reminded me of true prophecy; the words do not come out of your understanding, they flow out of your spirit.

I said to her, "When you die, you don't have to spend eternity in a devil's hell."

Instantly, I knew by the Spirit of God she was in prison on death row. At first, she seemed to reject what I said, as if she saw no hope for herself. I told her how much God loved her and that Jesus died on the cross for her sins. I said to her, "Jesus paid the price so that you can spend eternity with Him."

Then, I asked her, "Don't you want to receive Him as your Savior?"

She said, "Yes."

I prayed a prayer of repentance that she repeated. She believed on the Lord Jesus Christ and was saved.

When we said, "Amen," she immediately sat up on the bed and wrapped her arms around me so tightly. She began to sob uncontrollably. I knew that it was a heartfelt prayer and she meant every word. She was truly forgiven.

The right side of her face was touching mine as she was hugging me. She whispered in my ear, "I didn't mean to kill her."

I said to her, "I know you didn't and Jesus doesn't hold it against you."

She held me only a few minutes, but there was so much accomplished in that hug. I knew something awesome had happened, but only God knows the magnitude of the weight that was lifted off her in that moment. Tears streamed down her face as she lay back on her bed after releasing me from the hug of power. I took a step backwards, and immediately I was back in my bed. (I had noticed that when I was ready to leave a place, I never turned to walk out. I always took a step backward and returned to my body.)

I began to weep because I knew she was on death row. I did not know why she was on death row, the Spirit did not reveal that. Nor did I know she had killed a "her" until she told me. Your sins and iniquities God will remember no more (Hebrews 8:12). I thought, "What if no one had gone to share Jesus with her? What if I had not overcome my fears and aborted the assignment?" Praise God I did not! I am looking forward to seeing her when I get to heaven.

There are untold hundreds of people like that woman, on death rows, in hospitals, and stuck in other traps of life with no hope of going to heaven. They can be reached with the message of love and their eternal destiny be changed if Christians learned to be spiritually transported. Again, that is why I wrote this book. I hope in some way it will serve as a message that this can be done, and it will be a guide to help others know how to be translated.

There back at home in my bed, I could still feel that woman's arms around me and her face up against mine as if it was imprinted in my flesh. This feeling was different from my other experiences and made me wonder if I had been translated spirit, soul, AND BODY. I know bodily translation is possible because the Spirit of God caught away Phillip and he was found in another place (See Acts 8:39).

This experience made me pray even more. I couldn't wait until nighttime when the busyness of my day was complete because I desperately wanted to be used of God again. By this time I lived to be used of God. I went to bed night after night expecting to be translated. I would tell my husband, "I'm going to minister to someone tonight." He would say, "Okay, maybe the Lord will let you." Every night I would lie in bed and intentionally focus. I had learned that I had spiritual eyes, and if they were open I could see. Therefore, I lie in bed waiting with my spiritual eyes open, hoping God would show me something. At times I would see a person or place or thing. If I did, then there would be something like a magnetic tug pulling me toward the object. At times I would actually feel myself leave my body, and other times I would just appear there. Sometimes I was blessed to see the scenery along the way. On certain occasions, in a twinkle of an eye, I would arrive at my destination. But each time, I had to agree to go by focusing on whatever God showed me, or by submitting to the Father's will as I felt myself leave my body.

I resolved that I was not going to give up! I really wanted to fly, and I knew the Holy Spirit would help me get it right.

7

Completed Assignments

The Parking Lot

On another occasion, while at my home I saw in the Spirit a man lying in a parking lot. As I focused, I came up out of my body and flew to my destination. As I descended toward the man, I noticed there were several cars and people in the parking lot, but no one seemed to notice him nor me. He was lying beside a car. I knelt beside him, put my right hand under his head and lifted it a little, and declared, "You will live and not die in Jesus' Name!" I did not know what had happened to him. It seemed that he had suffered a heart attack and maybe was dead. But I knew he would live! As signs of life returned, I knew another divine assignment was complete in the Mighty Name of Jesus. The next thing I knew, I was back in my room. I walked over to my bed and went back into my body.

The Motorcycle

I was so excited! My prayers were being answered. The Holy Spirit was teaching me how to function on these assignments. I not only could control myself, but I could control other things when the need arose.

On another occasion, the Spirit carried me up a mountain. I followed a sharp, crooked road like those roads I have seen in the Smoky Mountains of Tennessee. On my left, I could see the lights of the city below as I ascended the mountain. Up ahead, I saw someone on a motorcycle. To my surprise, I descended and sat on the back of the motorcycle without causing any disturbance! As we started down the mountain, we quickly approached a very steep curve that I knew, without supernatural help, the rider was not going to make. From the back of the bike, I was able to lean to keep the rider from having an accident. We made the curve! Finally, as the bike was slowing down, it hit a bump that caused me to be ejected in a backwards flip off of it.

I knew my assignment was complete.

The 18-Wheeler

> *"This charge I commit unto thee, son Timothy, according to the prophecies which went before on thee, that thou by them mightiest war a good warfare;" 1 Timothy 1:18*

Just because a prophetic word is spoken into your life doesn't necessarily mean that it will automatically happen. You have to remind God of what He has spoken to you; not because He has forgotten, but rather to remind you of what He has said so that you won't let it slip away from you.

While writing this book, I received prophecies telling me that I must finish it before I can "move on to the next phase." I do not know all that entails, but I trust the Holy Spirit to show me the way.

I have noticed my experiences thus far have occurred after having prayed in the Spirit. I have always known that praying in tongues is a doorway into the deeper spiritual things of God. Now, I am convinced it also opens the door for my trips to do my special assignments. I do not say, nor do I believe, that it is the only way to have such an experience. I am only speaking from my past experiences.

A quick look into the Old Testament, which records the time before the Holy Spirit was given, will show that there were those who were spiritually transported. Therefore, these type of spiritual experiences are not limited to praying in tongues. I only know it is the way mine began. I have learned to simply relax, and in doing so I can submit to what the Holy Spirit wants my spirit to do.

One night while lying in bed after I had prayed in the Spirit for a while, I began to see a vision. At the same time, I noticed my spirit leaving my body. As it made its exit through the top of my natural head, I realized I was seeing the vision with my spiritual eyes because the vision continued as I exited my body. Again I tell you, the spirit of man is an amazing creature!

The Bible says,

> "For what man knoweth the things of a man, save the spirit of man which is in him? Even so the things of God knoweth no man, but the Spirit of God." 1 Corinthians 2:11

This verse seemed to come alive to me through the things I have learned about my spirit-man.

As this experience continued, my head pointed westward. Suddenly, I shot like a rocket through the headboard of my bed, through the wall, and through the living room of the house! Then, all of a sudden, I began to go upward.

I felt an awesome feeling of freedom! With an amazing ability, I turned flips and other similar aerobatic stunts. Next, I began to fly horizontally. Never had I experienced anything like it! I have always loved to ride roller coasters, bungee jumping, etc. But the thrill of this far exceeded them all. I think the Lord allowed me to experience these amazing things just to let me know how magnificent of a creature we truly are, and what we (our spirits) are capable of doing.

Soon, the reality of the darkness around me made me remember I needed to keep my eyes open. As I was uncertain if they were open or not, I reached up with my right hand and touched my eyes to make sure they were really open. They were.

Total darkness surrounded me. I was flying an unknown course, and it was too dark for me to see anything at all. As in the past, I fully relied on the Holy Spirit to lead me to my destination.

Finally, the darkness of night passed and I was now in light of day. I did not know my geographical location. I landed in an upright position, and I knew that I needed to walk in the direction I faced without turning.

I came to an eighteen-wheeler truck that had been in an accident. I walked to the passenger side of the truck while carefully looking everything over.

Seeing nothing that required my help, I asked the Lord, "What is it?"

I walked down the side, around the back of the truck, and up the other side before I saw him. A man lying on the ground near the front tire. I also noticed someone slumped over in the cab of the truck. I knelt down beside the man on the ground. He was lifeless. I immediately commanded him to live and not die.

I said, "You will live and not die, in Jesus' Name!"

I decreed it boldly three times before I saw his chest begin to move as breath came back into him. I knew he was going to be alright and my assignment was finished. I stood upright and took a step backwards. It was as though I simply stepped through a veil and was back in my bedroom. Almost instantly I could feel my spirit going back into my body.

I felt really bothered that the Lord did not have me minister to the person inside the truck. I did not know if he was unconscious or dead. I only knew my assignment ended and the other person remained in the hands of a just God.

A point for the reader to understand is these missions are strictly and totally under the leadership of the Holy Spirit, even though at times I was seemingly "pre-programmed" and knew what to do without being told. Yet, at other times, I would have to inquire of the Lord.

8

Time Travel

"Jesus said unto him, If thou canst believe, all things [are] possible to him that believeth." Mark 9:23

One Sunday night a minister came to our church to bring a message from God to us. During the message, he talked about going back in time and talking to a Prophet who had already gone home to be with the Lord. I was intrigued by his testimony. The thought came to my mind, "Is that possible?"

What would be the point of him sharing that experience if it's not true? Why would he lie?

These were some of the questions that flooded my mind when he shared that story. I know there is no time in eternity, and I also know that God is no respecter of person, but would He do that for me? I simply reminded the Lord of a prophecy that He had given me. He said, "You are liken unto Aimee Semple McPherson." My husband and I left church and went home. When we were in bed, I said to him, "I'm going back in time to one of Aimee Semple McPherson's services. I want the Lord to show me what he wants me to know about her before I research her on the internet." My husband responded, "Well, you received that prophetic word about her and all things are possible with God."

I finally went to sleep and dreamed that I was sitting in a living room. The living room was not mine nor one that I had seen before. In the living room I saw an antique television. I watched myself get up off the couch and go over to the television. I was then drawn into the television. The next thing I knew, I stood outside of a building. I noticed a blue sign off to the left as I walked in. I did not read the sign, I only caught a glimpse of it, but I am sure it told of the revival services that were going on there. When I stepped into the building, to my surprise, it was an arena. I stood there in awe of what I was seeing. The Presence of God electrified the place! Gospel music was being amplified through bullhorn speakers that were hung in different places in the arena. The arena was packed with people. I did not see anyone standing; everyone was seated and eagerly awaiting the opening of the service.

It was awesome in that place! Suddenly, I was drawn to a lady sitting in the front of the arena. She had on a white dress and a white hat. She, all of a sudden, began to be magnified as if she was drawn in by the lens of a camera. I knew it was Aimee McPherson. I said to myself, "It is possible! It is possible to go back in time." My only regret is that I did not get to hear her preach the Word of God. I did not want to leave that arena. I later saw her picture on the internet. That lady was indeed Aimee Semple McPherson. Yes, all things are possible with God!

Father had answered my prayer! I am sure this will be hard for some to believe, but I lie not--it happened. Ask and ye shall receive! Learn to trust the One Who is leading you even if it's not the norm. During those times there are supernatural downloads of information that would take years to learn and teach. I know I received more than I can share now. If one doubts it is possible to look back into time by the Spirit of God, let him read John 17:3-5,

> "And this is life eternal, that they might know thee the only true God, and Jesus Christ, whom thou hast sent. I have glorified thee on the earth: I have finished the work which thou gavest me to do. And now, O Father, glorify thou me with thine own self with the glory which I had with thee before the world was."

Jesus is praying there and He transcends time. He comes up out of time and looks one way, and says, "Father, glorify me with the glory I had with you before the foundation of the world." Then He looks the other way and says, "I have finished the work you sent me to do." But how can He say that when He had not had his beard plucked out, nor His back beaten, nor gone to the cross, nor resurrected from the dead? Yet, He declares, "I have finished the work you sent me to do." He had not only looked back in time, but forward into the future.

Oh, sons and daughters of God! Please hear me. The spirit realm is an awesome realm and you have access to it! Can any true son or daughter of God doubt the words of God?

9

Purging Pride

Pride goeth before destruction, and an haughty spirit before a fall.
Proverbs 16:18

Eventually, I got to a place where I was feeling really good about accomplishing my assignments. If I sensed fear in any way, I quickly reminded myself that God had not given me the spirit of fear. I longed for each time God would use me. I thought about being translated with great anticipation.

I wanted people to know how God was using me, as if I was some great person who had arrived.

One day, I sat with a group of people at church and discussed the message of the previous service. When there was a moment of silence, I told them about being translated and the assignments Father had sent me on. My story had nothing to do with the topic of discussion.

As we went our separate ways and I got quiet with myself, the Holy Spirit said to me, "Why did you share that?"

At first, I did not know how to answer, but the question made me ask myself, "Yeah, why did you share that?"

I then realized pride led me to share my translation experiences.

Pride is an ugly thing.

Proverbs 29:23 says,

> "A man's pride shall bring him low: but honour shall uphold the humble in spirit."

Pride will take you for a ride, and it will not take you where you want to go. I went before the Lord and confessed my pride about God using me in spiritual traveling. The translation experiences ceased at this point.

Oh, I was heartbroken! I wondered if Father would ever allow me to be used in this way again.

For a year and a half I hadn't gone to minister to anyone. I knew that I had to deal with the pride that was in my heart. I began to cry out to the Holy Spirit to help me remove the pride out of my heart. I knew that in order to be used of God I had to remain humble. Romans 8:13 says,

> "For if ye live after the flesh, ye shall die: but if ye through the Spirit do mortify the deeds of the body, ye shall live."

I knew to repent, but I really did not know how to pray to remove pride.

So, I gave myself over to the Holy Spirit. I ask him to help me uproot pride. I just prayed in tongues as he gave me the utterance. God has given us a way to remove everything in us that is not pleasing to Him. Once I admitted that I had a pride problem, I positioned myself in the best place because I was willing to get rid of it! Proverbs 16:18 reads,

> "Pride goeth before destruction, and a haughty spirit before a fall."

Hebrew number 7667 for the word destruction, sheber, means ruin. I was going to be ruined in this area if I had not allowed the Holy Spirit to help me.

> "In order to be used of God I had to remain humble."

It's only by His grace, that I am allowed to do these things. I am only a willing vessel who wants to be used mightily by God. If He wants me to go, I am willing. I am nothing without Him, and I am only doing things through Him. I must remain humble. I cannot exalt myself. The reason I chose to expose myself is to let you, the reader, know that if the Father chooses to use you in translation, preaching, laying hands on the sick, etc., you must remain humble. Whosoever humbles himself shall be exalted (by God) and whosoever exalts himself will be humbled (by God).

10

Hunger for More of God

"O taste and see that the LORD is good: blessed is the man that trusteth in him." Psalms 34:8

Many of the promises in the Word of God are conditional. For instance, Matthew 6:33 says,

"Seek ye first the kingdom of God and his righteousness and all these things will be added unto you."

Notice, seek ye first - if you seek the kingdom of God first then things are added to you.

"Draw nigh unto God and He will draw nigh unto you." James 4:8

You must first draw nigh to God. In other words, if you do your part first, then God will do His part. Just because God speaks into your life doesn't mean that it automatically happens. We have a part to do.

I believe you must have a hunger for the things of God.

The more hunger you have, the more you will be filled.

"The young lions do lack, and suffer hunger: but they that seek the

> LORD shall not want any good thing." Psalm 34:10

This makes me ask: How hungry are you for the things of God?

Are you hungry enough to seek Him with all your heart?

Are you hungry enough to say "No" to the things of this world so the Lord can have your undivided attention?

Are you hungry enough to push back your plate in order to humble your soul and get rid of doubt and unbelief?

Are you hungry enough to get out of bed in the early hours of the morning to allow the Holy Spirit help you pray out the plan of God for your life?

Just how hungry are you?

Psalm 107:9 says,

> "For he satisfieth the longing soul and filleth the hungry soul with goodness."

Do you want to be filled with the goodness of God?

These are some of the questions that I had to ask myself. I knew the Father had a spiritual path for my feet and I did not want anything to keep me from it. Therefore, I became willing to make the necessary sacrifices. Jesus said, If any will come after me, let him deny (say no to) himself, take up his cross daily and follow me (Luke 9:23). Let Father fill every longing and desire as you set yourself to pursue Him. He's waiting for you to take the first step. His Word ensures you to be more than a conqueror, therefore, you are able to conquer those things set to keep you from your goals. Allow the Holy Spirit to help you walk in God's fullness.

11

Out of Body/In Body

"For I know the thoughts that I think toward you, saith the Lord, thoughts of peace, and not evil, to give you an expected end."
Jeremiah 29:11

I awoke in the early hours one morning and spent time praying. After prayer, the Spirit of God talked with me. He said, "You know My authority. You have operated in My authority. Now, go forth in My authority and be no longer idle."

When He said "idle," I thought to myself, "Idle?" "Who's idle?"

I began to run through my mind all the things I had to do daily. The thought of all the things I involved myself in made me wonder how I was able to get them all done. I could honestly say my plate was full. The Holy Spirit interrupted my thoughts and said, "Yes, but how much of that is what others want you to do? How much of it is what you think you should be doing as a Pastor? And how much of it did I tell you to do?"

After thinking about what He just asked me, I realized I spent my time doing very little of what He had actually told me to do. I consumed my time with "do-good things," church-expected things, and self-things, but not a lot of God things.

With a repentant heart, I said, "God, if You will tell me or show me what You want me to do, I will do it."

After waiting for a while and not hearing Him speak, I went back to bed and quickly fell asleep. I then saw myself driving down an unfamiliar road. The road dead-ended and I had to turn right or left, but my car was going too fast to stop. I was headed into the woods, but I turned the steering wheel quickly, closed my eyes, and braced myself for the impact, but felt none.

> "Now, go forth in My authority and be no longer idle."

I opened my eyes, and to my surprise, my car was in flight. I noticed other cars flying also. I thought to myself, "Is this how it looks when God translates vehicles?"

Then, all of a sudden, I was out of my car and standing in a hospital.

I recognized my location to be the waiting room of the Anniston Regional Medical Center, in Anniston, Alabama. I stood there watching people come and go. Some coming in through the glass doors at the front, others sitting in chairs, and still others waiting on the elevator doors to open.

As the elevator delivered and received others in their place, I asked the Lord, "Which one? Who is it? Who do You want me to minister to?"

After waiting and waiting, I finally turned around to look the opposite way. I saw a man sitting down. I noticed his seat would accommodate two people, so I went over and sat down beside him. As I sat down, he reached and touched me. We looked at each other and our eyes seemed to lock together.

Then the Spirit caught me away.

I was carried from the hospital in Anniston to my bed in Piedmont in an instant.

This experience excited me. The Lord answered a prayer I had just prayed before I had gone to bed.

That settled it.

I was determined to go to the hospital.

The next day, I told my husband about the experience, and he agreed that I should go to the hospital. I went expecting to see the man I had seen the night before. The waiting room appeared much like I had seen it during my travel there in the early morning. People were coming and going, sitting and waiting, and using the elevator. But I did not see the man.

After a while, I asked the Lord, "Who is it? Who do you want me to minister to?" I continued people-watching. Finally, the Lord drew my attention to the front doors. I saw a woman wearing a pink shirt walk in.

My spirit came up and out of the top of my head causing my body to come into a standing position as the woman passed by me. I knew I was to follow her, so I walked behind her as she entered the elevator. She pushed the button for the eighth floor, and looked at me to know my floor.

I said, "That's good" and quickly started a conversation with her by asking her how she was doing. She seemed to be frustrated about something as she answered me, "I'm not doing too good today. My phone is almost dead, so I went down to my car to see if I had a charger, but I didn't. My husband is here in the hospital. He was diagnosed with a brain tumor, so I'm not doing well right now."

I said, "I will pray for you and your husband." She thanked me as the elevator doors opened.

She stepped off the elevator and I stepped off right behind her. I did not know what else to do at the moment, so I followed her down the hall. Finally, she reached her husband's room and went in.

I stood in the hall and prayed, "Lord, You've got to help me."

I knew what I had to do, so I took a deep breath and pushed the door open and walked in. The lady turned to see who had come in behind her. I didn't give her a chance to speak.

I quickly said, "Ma'am, I don't want you to think I was just following you, but the Lord wants me to pray for your husband, do you mind?"

The husband answered, "No, I don't mind."

I walked over to his bed, laid my hands on him, and commanded the tumor to leave his head with no adverse side effects. I could feel the power of God going into him. I also could feel it in the atmosphere and the couple could too.

As I finished praying, I looked at the woman; tears were flowing down her cheeks. She and her husband thanked me.

I said, "Thank Jesus, He's the One Who paid the price for your healing."

I left that room knowing something had taken place in that man's head. I knew that tumor had its orders and had no choice but to obey. I also knew I was in God's perfect will at that moment, and it felt great.

That event took place almost two years ago, and I am still going to the hospital weekly. I know God has a plan for each of us. It is up to us individually to seek God in order to know what His plan is for our lives. It is my belief that He wants to use each of us in our special assignment. All we have to do is ask, listen, and do.

After the event at the hospital, I understood that when God translated me there, He was preparing me to minister to the woman's husband and many others. He let me know that if I was obedient to Him and go, others would reach out to me and be healed. I have seen people give their lives to Jesus, and others healed and set free by the mighty power of God. All glory to Him!

12

No Fear In Love

"There is no fear in love; but perfect love casteth out fear: because fear hath torment. He that feareth is not made perfect in love."
1 John 4:18

I have never questioned God's love for me. From my earliest remembrance, I always knew God loved me. I have questioned a lot of things in life, but never my heavenly Father's love. On a Sunday morning in the month of January in 1983, I walked down a church aisle to meet Love. I will never forget how I felt when He wrapped His loving arms around me.

The thought of a God that loved the world so much He gave His only Son to save them made me want to meet Him. I walked down the aisle of Faith Temple Christian Center in Jacksonville, Alabama, stood at the altar, repented of my sins, and invited Jesus to live in my heart. What a glorious day! It is one that I will never forget.

I will never forget how love washed all my hurts away. I have disappointed Him many times since that morning, but nothing I could ever do will separate me from His awesome love.

So why should I fear? Fear feeds the enemy like faith pleases God. I have a promise from my God that He will never leave me nor forsake me.

I want to starve the enemy!

> "[Let your] conversation [be] without covetousness; [and be] content with such things as ye have: for he hath said, I will never leave thee, nor forsake thee." Hebrews 13:5

> "The LORD [is] my light and my salvation; whom shall I fear? the LORD [is] the strength of my life; of whom shall I be afraid?" Psalm 27:1

13

The Unknown

What if you leave your body and don't come back?

Are you not afraid?

What if this is really the devil and not God?

Many questions have come to my mind, like pestering gnats to frustrate my purpose. I knew that my encounters were not a common subject among church people.

Even though I wanted more than anything else to please God, I found myself fearing the unknown. There were no "How To" books on the subject, no "Ten Steps" messages. The few books I had read that mention translation were about people who got it right the first time. They went to where the Spirit took them, finished their assignment, and came back. They never told of any mistakes they made or even if they made any.

I knew the Holy Spirit would teach me how to fly. That was my prayer, "Holy Spirit teach me how to fly, teach me how to operate outside of my body." The Holy Spirit led me through the Word of God. He revealed Scriptures on translation to me. As I began to study these Scriptures, my soul became settled in knowing that God is still in the translation business.

Time with my Friend and Great Teacher calmed me. I said to myself, "So what if I don't come back, it'll be alright, I'll just go on to heaven." My new attitude seemed to make all the tormenting thoughts cease.

As I said before, hearing people testify of an out-of-the-body trip is not a common thing. Even though I knew it was God, I wanted the Bible to back up my experiences.

Therefore, I made a search through His Word to find out if anyone had ever had those kinds of experiences. They had. In 2 Corinthians, Apostle Paul gives a very clear account of a man being carried to the third heaven. He says he was not sure if the man was in his body or out of his body, but the account was sure and very detailed. This account made me feel better about my experiences. There were times when even though I knew I had left my body, I felt as though I was in my body. During those times, I found it difficult to tell if I had arrived at a place in-body or not. I could feel, smell, see, think, and talk. I could even fear. All my senses worked perfectly. My emotions definitely operated because many times I felt the pain of the individual I was sent to help.

1 Thessalonians 5:23 says,

> "and the very God of peace sanctify you wholly; and I pray God your whole spirit and soul and body be preserved blameless unto the coming of our Lord Jesus Christ."

From these verses, as I have referenced before, we can clearly understand that man is a triune being; he is a spirit, he has a soul, and he lives in a body. You are not going to be a spirit when you die. You are right now a spirit. You live in a body. You are not going to become an angel when you die and go to heaven to play a harp on some cloud. You are already a spirit. Your soul is your mind, will, and emotions. The Word of God does make the separation between spirit and soul. Hebrews 4:12 says,

> "For the Word of God is quick and powerful, and sharper than any two-edged sword, piercing even to the dividing asunder of soul, and spirit, and of the joints and marrow, and is a discerner of the thoughts and intents of the heart."

This truth has become so much clearer to me since I have traveled in the Spirit. The only thing that has been left behind is my body. One might think, "If the body is left, the feelings will be left also." That is not the case because your soul is the seat of all five senses. Therefore, your spirit and soul makes the trip together. That is not to say your body cannot come along, for surely there are Bible accounts of men being translated spirit, soul, and body. But for now, I discuss spirit and soul only because for the most part this has been the context of my experiences thus far.

I understand 2 Corinthians 12:2,

> "I knew a man in Christ above fourteen years ago, (whether in the body, I cannot tell; or whether out of the body, I cannot tell: God knoweth;)..."

The Word of God is the only thing that can make a separation of the spirit and soul of man. If I had not allowed the Word of God to make this distinction then I would have thought that the fear I was having was coming from my spirit (the real me) and not my soul. I had to renew my soul with the Word of God. So, I began to talk to my soul and tell it that 2 Timothy 1:7 says,

> "For God hath not given us (ME) the spirit of fear; but of power, and of love, and of a sound mind."

I began to confess this Scripture. I began to see myself entering the unknown without fear. This Word began its engrafting into my soul. When I was outside of my body, the moment I sensed fear I would quote the Word of God. It stabilized me.

I dwell in the secret place of the Highest and abide under the shadow of Almighty God.

The Lord is my light of my salvation whom shall I fear; the Lord is the strength of my life of whom shall I be afraid?

Perfect love casts out all fear.

I have been made perfect in His love.

"I could feel, smell, see, think, and talk. I could even fear."

14

Frequently Asked Questions

1. What is translation?

Translation is to transfer or transport from one place to another.

In Hebrews 11:5, by faith Enoch was translated that he should not see death; and was not found, because God translated him: for before his translation he had this testimony, that he pleased God.

This verse and other references show that people can be translated by the Spirit of God from one geographical place to another.

2. Is translation for today?

Absolutely! We have New Testament examples of people being translated. In Acts 8:39-40 it says,

> "when Philip and the Eunuch were come up out of the water, the Spirit of the Lord caught away Philip, that the Eunuch saw him no more: and he went on his way rejoicing. But Philip was found in Azotus: and passing through he preached in all the cities, till he came to Caesarea."

I have my own personal testimony of being translated and there are others in my church who have had translation experiences.

3. What is the purpose of being translated?

In Philip's experience, he was translated so that he could preach in other cities. The Holy Spirit helped him fulfill the Great Commission by translation. Translation is not for common, go-to-the-store travel, but I think I will call it Kingdom travel. By that I mean it is a way of travel when doing the work of the Kingdom of God.

4. What do you have to do to make it happen?

As for my experiences, I acknowledge that I am like the wind as Jesus told Nicodemus in John 3. I ask the Holy Spirit to take me wherever He would like for me to go. I make myself available by praying about my assignment and expect it to happen. I don't know when, but I wait on the Holy Spirit.

5. Do you travel by the Spirit or just appear in those places?

In my experiences, both have happened. There were times that I was aware of passing over bodies of water, mountains, etc. Then, there have been times that I just appeared in the place. I believe that it is whichever way the Holy Spirit chooses for you to go.

6. Can people that are not born again be translated?

These things belong to the children of God. However, God did under the Old Covenant translate people. For example, 2 Kings 5:25, 26 says,

> "But he went in, and stood before his master. And Elisha said unto him, Whence comest thou, Gehazi? And he said, thy servant went no whither. And he said unto him, went not mine heart (spirit) with thee, when the man turned again from his chariot to meet thee? Is it a time to receive money, and to receive garments, and olive yards, and vineyards, and sheep, and oxen, and menservants, and maidservants?"

I believe that the Prophet Elisha was actually translated by the Spirit to see these things take place.

In Ezekiel 37:1,

> "The hand of the LORD was upon me, and carried me out in the spirit of the LORD and set me down in the midst of the valley which was full of bones, and caused me to pass by them round about: and, behold, there were very many in the open valley; and, lo, they were very dry."

In 1 Kings 18:12,

> "And it shall come to pass, as soon as I am gone from thee, that the spirit of the LORD shall carry thee whither I know not; and so, when

I come and tell Ahab, and he cannot find thee, he shall slay me: but I thy servant fear the LORD from my youth."

These Scriptures indicate it was a common thing for people to be translated. This appears to be truth because Obadiah knew that God could translate Elijah.

7. Can others be translated with you?

Yes, in John 6:21, "Then they willingly received him into the ship: and Immediately the ship was at the land whither they went." Notice the word, "immediately."

8. Are all your faculties working when you are out of your body?

Yes, in Luke 16:19-24 is the account of the rich man who died and went to hell. In hell, he could see, feel, talk, and his emotions were intact. We know this because he described his torment. When you are out of your body, no matter where you are, your senses will still function.

9. Do you feel alone when you are translated?

No, I have never felt alone. I have a promise that God would never leave me nor forsake me, and I believe that to be true in-body or out-of-body.

10. Do you have to speak in tongues to be translated?

No, but praying in tongues helps you to pray out the perfect will/plan of God for your life. I believe praying in tongues is a doorway into the realm of the supernatural. And you build up yourselves on your most holy faith by praying in the Holy Ghost, which is much needed to accomplish the work of the mission you are sent to do.

11. What do I do if it never happens for me?

Never say "never." Just say, "I'm available." Continue anticipating. Live in expectation. Do not become weary of doing good. There are people in this world that will only be reached through supernatural means. God does not want them to perish without Him. Continue pursuing Him--not spiritual travel--Him. He is faithful and will use you mightily.

15

Testimonies From Others

Aaron's Testimony

Some people have simply heard my experience and took it to heart, which resulted in them having similar experiences. At one of our weekly men's meetings at our church, the women were invited to come. Our men's meetings are described as round table discussions of the deep things of God. This particular meeting gave way to hear about my experiences. I simply explained the things covered in this book, and how God can take those that are willing and yield to Him.

My son, Aaron, was in attendance that night and heard what I had to say. He stayed after service and asked a few more questions, mainly wanting to understand what he needed to do to begin to take spiritual trips. The next afternoon, he was on his way home from work when he had a traveling experience. The following is his words describing how the Lord took him.

> *I heard someone on the radio talking about how a dictator of another country was holding some Christian missionaries as prisoners. He was torturing and threatening to execute these missionaries.*
>
> *My heart hurt for the missionaries and for the nation's people. Several things ran through my mind:*

I thought of the times that I had heard my dad say, "There will be people who will appear past security and declare to political leaders what God has to say and be gone."

I thought about what I had heard the night before, thinking, "La Vance could go declare something like that, if God would just send her."

A holy anger rose up in me and I said, "God you should send someone to set that tyrannical dictator straight!"

It was then God asked me, "Would you go?!"

The light in front of me turned red, and I began to pray in the Spirit. My love, anger, and willingness had driven me to prayer, not really knowing what was about to happen. I just wanted God to move for those unfortunate people being hurt by the evil leader. As I prayed in the Spirit the strangest thing started to happen. I was taken!

I did not feel myself leaving my body, but rather felt myself walking. I was walking through a place where the atmosphere seemed distorted and somewhat blurred, as if I was walking through water. As I walked forward, I found myself moving through what looked like a screen of water into a room where everything was crystal clear. I have had many God-given visions where I have seen things in the Spirit, but this was no vision nor an imagination. It was very real. It was just as real as everyday life. I was no longer sitting in my car, I was standing in another room.

The room I was now standing in was a very large bedroom. All of the furnishings in this room were red, including the sheets and comforter on the bed. The bed was extremely large, estimated to be the size of two king-size beds pushed together. The bed had large decorative posts at each corner. I noticed a man lying on his stomach with his left arm embracing a pillow. The man wore a silky pair of silver pajama pants and no shirt. I could not help but notice that the man's skin was quite pale and ashy.

I felt a forceful tongue begin to roll out. As I was speaking in tongues, the sleeping man awoke and turned to look at me. The man seemed terrified, almost petrified, staring with his mouth wide open, but not saying a word. It was obvious that the words that I was speaking were in the man's dialect, and that the man understood everything being said, even though I had no idea what I said. The more I spoke, the tighter the man's grip on his pillow became. Finally, the man threw his pillow, which passed through me as if I had no substance. I finished the message that I was sent to give, and then, as the man began to call out in an unknown language, everything became distorted again. This time, when it cleared up I found myself sitting back in my car and the light in *front of me turning green.*

I was so shocked by what I had just experienced, that I could not wait to check it all out. As odd as this may sound, I was not even sure what the dictator looked like, so I whipped out my phone while driving and Googled a picture of the dictator I heard the radio announcer discuss moments earlier. Guess what, there was the man I had just awaken from his sleep! I clicked on a news article that explained the leader had been very sick recently. To me this explained his pale ashy skin.

After this experience happened, Aaron immediately called his dad to tell of his experience. The following Monday morning, his dad told the group of pastors and prayer warriors who meet weekly about Aaron's experience. Then, the next Monday, one of the pastors came with a reliable article that described the dictator's bedroom in very similar detail to Aaron's experience. Both Aaron and the article agreed on the size and description of the bed.

Chris's Testimony

While lying in bed, I was awakened and felt the need to pray. So, I started praying for me and Shante, my fiancée, because we weren't feeling well. I prayed for our healing and started praying that I would know the call God has placed on my life. I also prayed that the gifts of the Holy Spirit would start manifesting themselves in my life.

As I was praying in the Spirit, I started hearing others praying in the Spirit also. All of a sudden, I was standing over a body at a car wreck. I don't recall what kind of car it was or if it was a male or female, but I knew the exact place of the wreck. This entire time I was praying in the Spirit, and then I got the interpretation. I began to declare, "You will not die, you shall truly live, so turn from your ways and follow me."

When I awoke the next day, I remembered the experience. I was familiar with the place where the wreck had happened; it was on my way to work. I told the person that rode to work with me about my experience. When we got to that location, I could see that there had been a wreck because of the skid marks, bent over stop sign, and other evidence that a wreck had taken place.

This experience reminded me of when La Vance told the story about going to the prison out-of-body to minister to someone. I know without a doubt that it also happened to me.

Angel's Testimony

When I was praying, all of a sudden I thought I was in a dream. I started to travel in the sky. At first, it was dark, but I could see the moon, and I could see the trees. I went over what appeared to be a lake. And at the end of that lake, there was a gazebo. A little bit farther, there was a house. I went into the house, but it was set up like a doctor's office. I went into a patient's room. She had a tumor on her elbow. I prayed for the tumor to go and then I floated back out. And then back to my room.

16

Prayer and Activation

I hope this book has inspired you to want the Holy Spirit to use you in the same way. If so, you will want to know how.

One key I have learned is to focus and to stay focused.

During my training period, I quickly realized that if I lost focus in the slightest way, I would abort the mission. Fear was always a major issue and was designed to distract me, causing me to lose focus. If for any reason I feared, I would feel myself descending. Focus is very important!

If I were to give you steps to being translated, the first would be to pray the prayer I have prepared for you on page 71 and then pray in the Spirit to cover your next trip. We don't always know we are about to be translated. So, I make it a practice to daily pray in the Spirit to cover my next trip. I want to be ready when the time comes.

After knowing I have covered my trip with prayer, I will simply submit my will to the Lord's will by saying, "Holy Spirit, I am ready to go wherever you want me to go, and do whatever the next assignment is."

I begin to look in the Spirit for a focusing point. I wait to see what the Holy Spirit will show me and what assignment He has waiting for me. I choose to put my "natural in neutral," because I know God wants to use the faculties and emotions of my spirit to communicate with me. Just as He gave the body the five senses (i.e. sight, hearing, smell, taste, and touch), so has He given the spirit senses for operating in the spiritual realm.

For example, I may see an ocean liner. I stay focused on the ship, and I might then be drawn toward it. I will not let anything cause me to lose my focus. If I do, all is lost and the ocean liner will fade away, and nothing will happen.

But if I stay focused, I will be drawn to the ship, and once on board I will know why I am there. Again, I must not let fear or anything else steal my focus. Then, the super-miraculous begins. I know what I am there to do and how to accomplish it.

Someone once asked me if the trip was long or short. Did I see any scenery? My answer is this: sometimes I am instantly there, other times I am aware of the travel time in different ways. For instance, I have been very much aware of the wind blowing on my face and through my hair. Once I saw a river below me as I flew above it, following it like it was my path to where I was going. Therefore, the travel time is as the Holy Spirit wills.

Please understand, you--the real you--is a spirit. You live in a body. If God sends you on an assignment, the moment you submit your super-miraculous experience begins. If your spirit goes without your body, you will not feel any different than you do right now as far as whether you are in or out of your body. Remember, the times I was sent to minister to people I was tangible. They were able to touch me, hug me, and speak to me. I was able to see, hear, and feel.

So, prepare to trust the Holy Spirit and stay focused regardless of what happens around you. In my experience, I was seen by only those to whom I was to minister.

The whole purpose of translation is to do God's bidding--not to just experience translation. You will find that you will know what to do as if you were programmed by the Holy Spirit. By that I mean there will be a knowing inside of you. But, if for some reason you do not know, you can do what Scripture tells us to do under any circumstance: Ask the Lord and He will let you know.

> "And all things, whatsoever ye shall ask in prayer, believing, ye shall receive." Matthew 21:22

Prayer of Activation

Dear Heavenly Father, I thank You for Your Word. Your Word is Truth. Jesus said, "The wind bloweth where it listeth, and thou hearest the sound thereof, but canst not tell whence it cometh, and wither it goeth: so is everyone that is born of the Spirit" (John 3:8). Therefore, I declare that I am born of the Spirit and I am like the wind. I go where You choose for me to go. I submit my entire being to Your will. Whenever and wherever You desire to translate me, I am willing and I am ready. Use me for Your glory. In the Name of Jesus Christ, I pray. Amen.

List of Referenced Scriptures

1 Kings 18:12

> And it shall come to pass, as soon as I am gone from thee, that the Spirit of the Lord shall carry thee whither I know not; and so when I come and tell Ahab, and he cannot find thee, he shall slay me: but I thy servant fear the Lord from my youth.

2 Kings 2:16

> And they said unto him, Behold now, there be with thy servants fifty strong men; let them go, we pray thee, and seek thy master: lest peradventure the Spirit of the Lord hath taken him up, and cast him upon some mountain, or into some valley. And he said, Ye shall not send.

2 Kings 5:25-26

> But he went in, and stood before his master. And Elisha said unto him, Whence comest thou, Gehazi? And he said, Thy servant went no whither.

> And he said unto him, Went not mine heart with thee, when the man turned again from his chariot to meet thee? Is it a time to receive money, and to receive garments, and oliveyards, and vineyards, and sheep, and oxen, and menservants, and maidservants?

Ezekiel 3:12

> Then the spirit took me up, and I heard behind me a voice of a great rushing, saying, Blessed be the glory of the Lord from his place.

Ezekiel 3:14

> So the spirit lifted me up, and took me away, and I went in bitterness, in the heat of my spirit; but the hand of the Lord was strong upon me.

Ezekiel 8:3

> And he put forth the form of an hand, and took me by a lock of mine head; and the spirit lifted me up between the earth and the heaven, and brought me in the visions of God to Jerusalem, to the door of the inner gate that looketh toward the north; where was the seat of the image of jealousy, which provoketh to jealousy.

Ezekiel 11:24

> Afterwards the spirit took me up, and brought me in a vision by the Spirit of God into Chaldea, to them of the captivity. So the vision that I had seen went up from me.

Ezekiel 37:1

> The hand of the Lord was upon me, and carried me out in the spirit of the Lord, and set me down in the midst of the valley which was full of bones,

Ezekiel 43:5

> So the spirit took me up, and brought me into the inner court; and, behold, the glory of the Lord filled the house.

Luke 24:36

> And as they thus spake, Jesus himself stood in the midst of them, and saith unto them, Peace be unto you.

John 3:8

> The wind bloweth where it listeth, and thou hearest the sound thereof, but canst not tell whence it cometh, and whither it goeth: so is every one that is born of the Spirit.

John 6:21

> Then they willingly received him into the ship: and immediately the ship was at the land whither they went.

John 20:26

> And after eight days again his disciples were within, and Thomas with them: then came Jesus, the doors being shut, and stood in the midst, and said, Peace be unto you.

Acts 8:38-40

> And he commanded the chariot to stand still: and they went down both into the water, both Philip and the eunuch; and he baptized him. And when they were come up out of the water, the Spirit of the Lord caught away Philip, that the eunuch saw him no more: and he went on his way rejoicing. But Philip was found at Azotus: and passing through he preached in all the cities, till he came to Caesarea.

1 Corinthians 5:3-4

> For I verily, as absent in body, but present in spirit, have judged already, as though I were present, concerning him that hath so done this deed, In the name of our Lord Jesus Christ, when ye are gathered together, and my spirit, with the power of our Lord Jesus Christ,

2 Corinthians 12:2-4

> I knew a man in Christ above fourteen years ago, (whether in the body, I cannot tell; or whether out of the body, I cannot tell: God knoweth;) such an one caught up to the third heaven. And I knew such a man, (whether in the body, or out of the body, I cannot tell: God knoweth;) How that he was caught up into paradise, and heard unspeakable words, which it is not lawful for a man to utter.

Colossians 2:5

> For though I be absent in the flesh, yet am I with you in the spirit, joying and beholding your order, and the stedfastness of your faith in Christ.

Revelation 1:10

> I was in the Spirit on the Lord's day, and heard behind me a great voice, as of a trumpet,

Revelation 4:2

> And immediately I was in the spirit: and, behold, a throne was set in heaven, and one sat on the throne.

Revelation 17:3

> So he carried me away in the spirit into the wilderness: and I saw a woman sit upon a scarlet coloured beast, full of names of blasphemy, having seven heads and ten horns.

Revelation 21:10

> And he carried me away in the spirit to a great and high mountain, and shewed me that great city, the holy Jerusalem, descending out of heaven from God,

Steps, Mistakes, and Successes in Following the Holy Spirit into Amazing Experiences

Date: _____

Experience: _____

_____
_____
_____
_____
_____
_____
_____
_____
_____
_____
_____
_____
_____
_____
_____
_____
_____
_____
_____
_____
_____
_____
_____
_____
_____
_____

Date: _____

Experience: _____
_____
_____
_____
_____
_____
_____
_____
_____
_____
_____
_____
_____
_____
_____
_____
_____
_____
_____
_____
_____
_____
_____
_____
_____
_____
_____
_____

Date: _____

Experience: _____

Date:

Experience:

Steps, Mistakes, and Successes in Following the Holy Spirit into Amazing Experiences

Date: _____

Experience: _____
_____
_____
_____
_____
_____
_____
_____
_____
_____
_____
_____
_____
_____
_____
_____
_____
_____
_____
_____
_____
_____
_____
_____
_____
_____
_____
_____
_____
_____
_____

Date: _____

Experience: _____

Steps, Mistakes, and Successes in Following the Holy Spirit into Amazing Experiences

Date: _____

Experience: _____

Made in the USA
Columbia, SC
27 March 2025